T0353703

Poem For Jesus

Sheralyn Turner

authorHOUSE®

AuthorHouse™
1663 Liberty Drive
Bloomington, IN 47403
www.authorhouse.com
Phone: 833-262-8899

Published by AuthorHouse 02/12/2025

ISBN: 979-8-8230-4305-2 (sc)
ISBN: 979-8-8230-4306-9 (hc)
ISBN: 979-8-8230-4304-5 (e)

Library of Congress Control Number: 2025902246

Print information available on the last page.

Any people depicted in stock imagery provided by Getty Images are models, and such images are being used for illustrative purposes only. Certain stock imagery © Getty Images.

This book is printed on acid-free paper.

Dedication

Heavenly Father, I pour out my heart through these poems, humbly offering them to You and asking for Your blessing on every word written here. I lift people both in my homeland and around the world, praying these words may guide, encourage, and bring hope to those who seek direction. Thank You for Your steadfast presence in my life, leading me according to Your perfect will and purpose.

These poems are dedicated to my children—Darrell, Darren, and Deanna—and my grandchild, who are still awaiting her arrival. May they always remember that God's love truly spans from everlasting to everlasting.

Thank you.

Introduction

The author explores her spiritual journey and personal growth through poetry born from the challenges and hardships she has faced over the years. Through prayer and meditation, she began journaling her deepest thoughts, allowing her life experiences to shape and inspire her writing. She reflects on how aging has deepened her introspection, leading her to a place of surrender that has strengthened her faith and fostered personal growth. Each poem vividly captures her pain and struggles, employing descriptive imagery to paint a rich and detailed portrait of her life, creating a deeply immersive and impactful experience for the reader.

The poems she writes come to her during Bible study and Sunday mornings in church, often described as a rush of voices or feelings, which she attributes to Jesus speaking through the Holy Spirit. This inspiration compels her to write fervently, sometimes questioning if what she is experiencing is real. Yet, the more she delves into the Bible, the more convinced she becomes that God wants her to share these messages.

As a parent, the author's greatest desire is for her children to serve God and feel His unconditional love. She expresses that her relationship with God has been a source of peace, guidance, and correction, emphasizing that God is central to her life. Her writings are a testimony to how God has saved her family many times, and her hope that these poems will impact others' faith and their eternal future. She encourages readers to remain steadfast in their faith and seek God, promising that His blessings will follow those who live by His commandments and statues.

Contents

A prayer of thanksgiving

Thank **you** for your strength to bear my cross,
Thank you for the revelation you have given me.
Thank you, Father God, for giving me the PUSH.
Thank you for the course of correction.
Thank you for putting me back on the right track.
To where you are taking me.
I am grateful for you inspiring me to write these poems.
And bring them to life.
Your, inspiring words, your dreams, and visions.
That was imparted to me.
Will not be put on the shelves or be ignored.
Thank You for not giving up on me.
Thank you for being a constant source in my life.
When my strength falters, you are there.
When I am broken, I know you are there to carry me.
May my experiences about you be of gratitude and sacrifice.
Thank you for loving me, I am so grateful.

Life has not always been easy for me, and there were times when offering a prayer of gratitude felt almost impossible. Yet, I've come to realize that giving thanks, even during pain, has been a source of healing. Now, I choose to be thankful for my past struggles, failures, losses, challenges, and even illnesses. I'm deeply grateful to the Holy Spirit for giving me the strength to say "thank you" boldly, even when facing difficulties.

When facing challenges, or disappointment, do you still offer up praises of gratitude to God?

REFLECT
YOU ARE THANKFUL FOR.

YOUR PERSONAL PRAYER.

John 1:1 - In the beginning was the Word, and the Word was with God, and the Word was God.

Where God met me

When God met me, I was reading Genesis.
He asked my daughter why you are crying.
Why are you alone, where is everyone?
Why are you not reading Exodus?
You should be leaving on your journey.
Hurry, hurry please, and turn the corner.
So that you can learn Leviticus and numbers
These are the books explaining the sacrificial system.
Teaching you how you can learn to worship and go into leadership.
I hesitated and stopped; O Lord where are you taking me now?
He said to me you are on your way to meet Deuteronomy.
Where you can go over to see the promised land
I grew strong and courageous. Because God
said Jesus is there do not be afraid
I finally reached over but God said my dear, there is more to see.
I ponder, I wonder what He is saying.
He said you need to find the light I told me about.
Then I remembered, a long time ago I Listen to
the words of the prophets and scholars.
Saying the light of the world is coming, and he shall be called.
wonderful counselor, mighty God, everlasting father, prince of peace
Finally, as I rest on the rock there appears a bright light shining at me.
I was amazed, I felt peace,
The joy I needed in Genesis is here.
The lights said, my dear, you do not need to
run anymore, the light is here.
His peace and his presence are all I need.
Finally, I reached the gospel of Jesus who fulfilled the Old
Testament prophecy and history change history forever

I've discovered that reading God's Word daily lays the foundation for a successful and fulfilling life. I view the Bible as a priceless gift from God—one that invites me to read, reflect, and meditate on its truths. By focusing my heart on His Word, I make space for the Holy Spirit to dwell within me. When I stay consistent and attentive, I receive fresh encounters from the Holy Spirit each day, empowering me to live with renewed strength.

Where were you when you recognize God's presence in your life, or what situation or place you felt the presence of God?

REFLECT

_____

_____

_____

_____

_____

_____

YOUR PERSONAL PRAYER

_____

_____

_____

_____

_____

_____

Revelation 1:3 "Blessed is the one who reads the words of this prophecy and blessed are those who hear it and hold on to the things written in it, because the time is near."

December Hands

Oh Lord thank you for opening the last chapter of December.
I envision your hands writing your words in the last
chapter, watching, as you carefully turn each page.
Meticulously taking your time, hoping that your words will be accepted.
The Lord said to write down your words for my people to read.
Each page is a day covered with hope for me and your people.
Each page is filled with love for my people.
Oh God, I see you crying over December.
I see you taking the arms of righteousness, and grace.
Wrapping it about each day, stretching out your arms
Wrapping it around your people and your church.
I see you Father God opening your deep well of forgiveness.
Telling your flocks to come and thirst no more.
Knowing that December is the final chapter in your book.
Symbolizes a new beginning and changes its appearance.
Changing all things around us for our good.

I remind myself that God establishes my steps and desires me to live according to His divine will and purpose. By aligning my life with His plans, I can walk in faith and fulfillment, trusting He guides me every moment of the way.

Have you ever envisioned God's fingers writing on your paper? What are your thoughts.

REFLECT

_____

_____

_____

_____

_____

_____

YOUR PERSONAL PRAYER

_____

_____

_____

_____

_____

_____

_____

_____

_____

_____

Psalm 59:16 "But I will sing of your strength, in the morning I will sing of your love; for you are my fortress, my refuge in times of trouble.

The strength of my life

The love of God exceeds everything about me.
The hope of God transcends my life.
The wisdom of God opens every closed door.
The heart of God marries me to his will.
The grace of God carries me forward.
The mercy of God helped me to stay focused.
My faith in God pushes me to higher heights.
The fear of God teaches me not to fear.
The strength of God holds and strengthens me when I am in trouble.
The Kingdom of God, Brings me in his closeness.
My confidence in God motivates me to my destiny.
The vision of God let me see beyond my fears and shortfalls.
The presence of God Gives me the courage to wait.
The courage of God teaches me not to be afraid.
The dwelling place of God gives me a place to rest.
The community of God keeps me grounded and in check.
He is the strength of my life, whom shall I be afraid of?

> **I pursue the Lord and His strength, seeking Him continually and trusting in His unwavering presence. Through faith, I confidently rely on Him, for He reminds me not to be discouraged—He is my God. In moments of weakness, He provides me with His strength; if I feel lost, He guides me. Challenges may arise, but with His support, I will overcome every obstacle.**

Have you ever asked why me? Have you ever seen yourself losing hope, in your marriage, on your job, your prayer life and during sickness? Write your thoughts. Don't loose hope, God never give up on you.

REFLECT

_____

_____

_____

_____

_____

YOUR PERSONAL PRAYER

_____

_____

_____

_____

_____

_____

_____

_____

_____

God's Cry

Wide is the earth and deep are my words.
I send my words to multiply you. To the people who hear my cry.
I send my words to anyone who will listen.
In ancient times I called on Abraham, Isaac,
Jacob, and Moses who heard me.
The word needs to be practiced; it needs to be heard.
Oh, do I not say I love you; do I not weep and wail?
The world is blue, I AM Blue, and the whale is blue.
I make time, I take time, I develop time, and time is mine.
My words are resting on a cushion, gathering dust.
Stand up dust off my word, go, hurry the word is calling you,
Feed my word to my people, answer my call.
Bring in the harvest so that I can rejoice.

God's Word should be read, studied, memorized, and deeply meditated upon. The Holy Spirit draws me closer to Him through His Word, transforming my heart and mind. Scripture is a powerful tool for teaching, training, and guiding us in truth and righteousness. Though I had always taken God's Word seriously, I realized there was more to discover. I intentionally immersed myself in it, continuously praying and seeking God for more profound revelation.

After praying one morning, I heard a voice, saying start to write. This is what I heard, and I obeyed, and I just couldn't stop writing. Have you ever experienced this? God visitation is different to everyone.

REFLECT

_____

_____

_____

_____

_____

_____

YOUR PERSONAL PRAYER

_____

_____

_____

_____

_____

_____

_____

_____

_____

_____

Jeremiah 15:16 says, "Your words were found, and I ate them; and your words became to me a joy and the delight of my heart, for I am called by your name, O LORD, God of hosts.".

The written word

The written word of God is the food.
It nourishes your body.
Just like you need food to eat.
God's word is food.
Oh, where can I find the written word of God?
Oh, where is it?
It is not hidden, it is not too far to find,
it is not hard to read, or where is it?
I look over The Valley,
I look over the deep sea,
oh where, oh where is it?
I know it is right here.
It is everywhere.
God's word is here, look come,
Oh, look my people, it is in your hands.
It is on the shelves.
It is in the airways, it is on social media.
The Written word of God should be in you.

I know it is essential to seek God's written word with dedication and sincerity. I pray with conviction, trusting that God rewards those who diligently and earnestly seek Him. He promises that those who seek will indeed find.

The word of God can nourish you in many ways. Reflect on some ways the word has nourished you.

REFLECT

_____

_____

_____

_____

_____

YOUR PERSONAL PRAYER

_____

_____

_____

_____

_____

_____

_____

_____

_____

_____

John 8:12 "When Jesus spoke again to the people, he said, 'I am the light of the world. Whoever follows me will never walk in darkness but will have the light of life.'"

God's light

Someone shouted where is the light?
Someone shout or where can it be?
Someone Shout, look at the darkness.
And shout at the darkness, where is the light?
The light that shines brightly.
The light that brings hope.
Where or where is that light
I search for that light.
I search in my heart for that light.
Some says I struggle for that light.
God says I gave you the light.
God says take the light and let it shine upon you.
The light of the world is Jesus Christ my son.
Someone shouted, I found the light.

God's light is my guide and revelation, showing me truth, salvation, and hope in my life. I pray daily, making it an essential part of my routine. I strive to foster fellowship and connect with other believers who share my goals and ideas about God. I want God's light to shine through my attitude, words, and deeds.

Reflect on how the true light can replace the darkness inside of you.
Write how you felt and how does it signify your relationship with God.

REFLECT

_____

_____

_____

_____

_____

YOUR PERSONAL PRAYER

_____

_____

_____

_____

_____

_____

_____

_____

_____

Matthew 10:32 "Whoever acknowledges me before others, I will also acknowledge before my Father in heaven."

Acknowledging God's name

Mighty is your name oh God.
Powerful is your name oh God.
Grace is your name oh God.
Peace is your name oh God.
Gracious is your name oh God.
Happy is your name oh God.
Wonderful is your name oh God.
Strong is your name oh God.
I acknowledge your name oh God.
In the bad good and differences.
I acknowledge your name in hope.
I acknowledge your name in Truth and spirit.
I acknowledge your name in my daily walk with you.
I acknowledge your name in your presence.
I will always acknowledge your name.

I've found that acknowledging God's name is vital in my faith. Whenever I praise, worship, or revere Him, I recognize His holiness and sovereignty. By listening to His voice in everything I do and wherever I go, I trust that He remains ever-present in my life.

> **Have you ever thought about asking God how can you honor his name when situation arises?**

REFLECT

_____

_____

_____

_____

_____

YOUR PERSONAL PRAYER

_____

_____

_____

_____

_____

_____

_____

_____

_____

James 1:5 If any of you lacks wisdom, you should ask God, who gives. Generously to all without finding fault, and it will be given to you.

Finding Wisdom

Wisdom is in here.
Wisdom is before you.
Where can I find wisdom?
Where can I look for wisdom?
I study Hard to find wisdom.
I travel far to find wisdom.
I seek scholars, and books trying to find wisdom.
A small voice whispers.
Don't you see wisdom as the written word of God?
Wisdom is in the holy book.
There it was, emerging in my hope, and in my life experiences.
Wisdom is in my qualities, where empathy is shown.
It is found in my studying, praying and staying
in communion with my God.
Wisdom will tell my story.

Throughout my adult life, I was always confused about wisdom. I prayed and prayed to God to give me wisdom. It was not until the Holy Spirit revealed that wisdom comes from God's mouth. Wisdom is His living and accurate word. This revelation brought me joy because I finally understood what it meant to please and trust God completely. God is the ultimate source of wisdom, knowledge, and understanding.

> **Have you ever taught about tapping into the wisdom of God?**

REFLECT

_____

_____

_____

_____

_____

YOUR PERSONAL PRAYER

_____

_____

_____

_____

_____

_____

_____

_____

_____

_____

Hebrews 13:21, "Equip you with everything good that you may do his will, working in us that which is pleasing in his sight, through Jesus Christ, to whom be glory forever and ever.

Equipped me

Equip me oh God with your love.
Equip me oh God with your shield of righteousness.
So that my heart is protected.
Equip me oh God with your strength.
With the gifts that you have given me.
Equip me oh God with the helmet of salvation.
That will bring my dreams and vision to life.
Equip me oh God with the word of faith.
So that my destiny will be fulfilled.
With your gifts oh, God according to your grace
So that you can collaborate with me to accomplish
What is pleasing to you?
Equip me, lord, with your peace, so that I can rest.
Because You will provide me with the tools I need.
To serve you faithfully.
Thank you, God, for equipping me.

As I face trials and temptations, I hold on to God's words, which teach me to believe that nothing is impossible by His hands. My only hope is to trust and obey God when I feel overwhelmed by trials and temptations. I know He will equip me with everything I need.

How has God use your past to equip you for what future?

REFLECT

_____

_____

_____

_____

_____

_____

YOUR PERSONAL PRAYER

_____

_____

_____

_____

_____

_____

_____

_____

_____

_____

_____

Colossians 3:2, "Set your minds on things that are above, not on things that are on earth."

Fields in my mind

I am troubled by the constant disturbance in my mind.
Each field in my mind appears rugged and not straight.
Tormented by the rocks and weeds.
Green is the field in my mind.
Fighting to stay focused.
Trying to destroy the negative weeds.
That are trying to break in.
Looking, waiting to be released, waiting for help.
Get ready negative weeds the time has come to be plucked.
The harvest is ripe, the promise is here.
Stay focused, and be consistent,
Waiting for the harvest to come.
Oh, fields of my mind keep waiting because victory will come.
The weeds that sow discord will be destroyed.
And victory will be won.

I used to torture myself, trying to find ways to control my thoughts. I know by preserving my thoughts I can stay focused on good and positive things. This is the key to allowing God's words to transform my mind. I strive to always align my thoughts and attitudes with God's will.

Reflect on a time or even now when your mind is so clutter with so many things that Gods presence cannot even enter. How did you handle it?

REFLECT

_____

_____

_____

_____

_____

YOUR PERSONAL PRAYER

_____

_____

_____

_____

_____

_____

_____

_____

_____

Corinthians 2:9."What no eye has seen, nor ear heard, nor the heart of man imagined, what God has prepared for those who love him."

Open my eyes and see.

Open my eyes and see the blessing of the Lord.
To behold his grandeur as He displays his wonder.
As the moonlit sky shows its splendor, for all eyes to see.
He opens my eyes and reveals the cross.
Revealing that I was blind but now I can see.
I looked up and there He was.
There my eyes behold, a shining light for all to see.
With an unveiled face He transforms my eyes.
To see His Kingdom far and wide.
Looking at the images, for all eyes to see.
Open my eyes oh God and see me, for all eyes to believe and see.
Awaiting the answer to my prayers.
Reviving hope beyond despair.

I seek to understand His truth when I ask God to open my eyes. I need to understand the revealed word of God for myself. I remember that revelation comes only from the Spirit of God. When I seek His presence and His will, whether as a literal opening of physical sight or a symbolic awakening to spiritual realities, I must submit myself to the transformative power of God.

When you are asking God to "open your eyes so that you can see" asked Him to show you what is hidden inside that needs to be reveal, so that you can enjoy the fullness of his glory.

REFLECT

_____

_____

_____

_____

_____

YOUR PERSONAL PRAYER

_____

_____

_____

_____

_____

_____

_____

_____

_____

1st Corinthians 6:19-20 (NIV): "Do you not know that your bodies are temples of the Holy Spirit, who is in you, whom you have received from God? You are not your own; you were bought at a price. Therefore, honor God with your bodies."

Becoming whole

I search high and low to find wholeness.
I search beyond my thoughts to find wholeness.
My soul searches for that wholeness
My body seeks permission for that wholeness.
Oh, how can I become whole?
To free the body of sickness.
A mind that is free from worries.
The hidden issues of life to be free.
All parts of the body make it whole.
The journey had just begun.
Surrender your thoughts.
Surrender to all your challenges.
Embrace all that is within you.
Fear, anxiety, and doubt will pass.
Brightness, joy, and curiosity welcome
Claim it, do not fear,
His desire is for you.
To have made you whole again.

I understand the importance of nourishing my body with wholesome foods and recognizing it as the temple of God. Being whole means that my spirit, soul, and body are all aligned in Jesus Christ. Throughout my life, I strive to live in service, obedience, surrender, and self-sacrifice to become whole in Him.

> Have you asked yourself what specific steps you need to start the process of becoming whole. God can mend the broken hearted and restore wholeness.

REFLECT

_____

_____

_____

_____

_____

YOUR PERSONAL PRAYER

_____

_____

_____

_____

_____

_____

_____

_____

_____

Psalm 19:1 says, "The heavens declare the glory of God; the skies proclaim the work of his hands."

Shop for God's glory

I wonder where to shop to find the glory of God.
Oh, how can I sit and consider the glory of God?
Oh, how I wonder how many times I should look for God's glory.
I am afraid I cannot find it.
Oh, where can it be?
It is in the moon's lit sky,
It is in the air we breathe.
It is in the joy we experience,
It is in our home where we live.
It is when we hear the birds singing,
It is when we see the different seasons.
It is when we see the sun shining its radiance of Light across the sky.
It is in the rainbow within clouds.
It is in the rain to nourish and feed the animals.
It is the food we eat to nourish us.
The Lord's glory is in the Wide deep vault Called the ocean.
The Lord's glory is in the wind he rides upon his cloud.
sending his messages to all who believe.
The glory of God is in your eyes to behold.

When I embody the principles of living righteously, glorifying God in everything I do, reflecting His image, worshiping, praising, sharing the gospel, and seeking to glorify Him in all areas of my life, I experience His glory. Living for God's glory is deeply personal and unique to my journey. I believe His glory is everywhere, and when I share and contribute to His glory, I actively participate in His kingdom on Earth.

Reflect on how you can glorify God. If you are having a difficult life, start glorifying God.

REFLECT

_____

_____

_____

_____

_____

_____

YOUR PERSONAL PRAYER

_____

_____

_____

_____

_____

_____

_____

_____

_____

_____

Deuteronomy 8:2-3"Remember how the Lord your God led you all the way in the wilderness these forty years, to humble and test you in order to know what was in your heart, whether or not you would keep his commands."

Circle around the wilderness

I circle in the wilderness, .I see my visions and dreams running away.
I cannot seem to hold on to them.
Where the shadows of darkness dwell.
I see challenges arising up in the wilderness.
I see my anxiety rising in the wilderness.
I see my fears rising in the wilderness.
I see stress, frustration, and pressure rising in the wilderness.
Oh, how can I manage these challenges in the wilderness?
In the wilderness, life will emerge.
Fertile land is transformed.
A new seed will grow, and a dimmer of light brings hope.
Guiding me on despite the challenges. Despite the pain I bear.
Hearing the ruffles of the leaves provides a life of hope.
Sending comfort and encouragement with the source of His strength.
For out of the wilderness there I will stand,
Only to meet up with God indeed.
In the wilderness he sent His messenger to search my heart.
And the shepherd to guide me forward.
The armor of grace to lead me on.
To a greater holiness towards my calling.

The wilderness experience has been a time of testing and refinement. It's a journey that has led to my personal growth, spiritual transformation, and turning my fears into peace. When I pray with faith and trust in God and His promises, I feel restoration and transformation take root in my life.

Have you ever found yourself in a situation where you know that if it weren't for the grace of God, you would not have gotten out of it?

REFLECT

_____

_____

_____

_____

_____

YOUR PERSONAL PRAYER

_____

_____

_____

_____

_____

_____

_____

_____

_____

_____

Proverbs 19:21 (NIV): "Many are the plans in a person's heart, but it is the Lord's purpose that prevails."

Desires of the heart

Desire of my heart where did you go.
Because it was given by God for you to see.
His plans and his desires center around my heart.
So that I can find delight in him.
Write it, speak it, and envision it.
Listen, read, devote time to him.
The heart knows when the time is right.
To drive the passion that I loved the most.
My purpose he knows.
Mysterious longings that cannot be satisfied.
Only he knows what he has made.
It is written on man's heart for him to find.
I dare not see him grieve.
I dare not break his heart.
I dare not leave his presence.
The sadness of his heart is too much for me to bear.

I believe the heart has many desires, but seeking God's will and acknowledging His purpose is the first step in aligning my desires and trusting in His plan for my life. When I focus on His guidance, I find peace and clarity in every decision.

> **Have you ever wondered if your desire of your heart is aligned up to the will of God?**

REFLECT

_____

_____

_____

_____

_____

YOUR PERSONAL PRAYER

_____

_____

_____

_____

_____

_____

_____

_____

Deuteronomy 8:2-3 "Remember how the Lord your God led you all the way in the wilderness these forty years, to humble and test you in order to know what was in your heart, whether or not you would keep his commands."

Search Me

Search me heavenly Father and see my heart.
Search me heavenly Father and see my thoughts.
Search me heavenly Father and see my beginnings.
Search me heavenly Father and see my sins.
Search me heavenly Father and see my groaning.
Search me heavenly Father and see my life.
Search me heavenly Father and see my cries.
Search me heavenly Father and see my lies.
Search me heavenly Father and see my emptiness.
Search me heavenly Father and see my wicked ways.
Search me heavenly Father and see my repentance.
My overflow is found in my Searching for my heavenly Father.

These verses express my desire for God to search, know, and examine my innermost thoughts, intentions, and desires. They reflect my prayerful attitude of openness and surrendering before Him, inviting His scrutiny and guidance in leading a righteous life.

> **Have You asked God what hidden areas in your heart that He wants to reveal so that you can start walking in his part.**

REFLECT

_____

_____

_____

_____

_____

YOUR PERSONAL PRAYER

_____

_____

_____

_____

_____

_____

_____

_____

John 5:14-15 (NIV): "This is the confidence we have in approaching God: that if we ask anything according to his will, he hears us. And if we know that he hears us—whatever we ask—we know that we have what we asked of him."

I pray for an answer

With a heavy heart do I pray
Oh Lord, answer me, I await dear Lord.
I pray with a confused mind, I await answer me, Lord.
I pray with a downcast soul, only you can listen.
For my soul only sees you, Lord.
My heart desires for you Lord.
As I continue to push through.
When I pray with all my strength, you will answer me.
When I pray for your mercy, you will answer me.
When I pray for peace in my mind, you will answer me.
When I pray to the Holy Spirit to come, the Lord does answer me.
O Lord, sometimes not the answer I expected.
But I will continue to praise you.
I will continue to believe in your promises,
even when I am unable to pray.
Oh, my Lord, only you know what is best for me.

These words highlight the promise and assurance that God hears and answers my prayers, when I seek Him with sincerity and faith, according to His will. His Word encourages me to approach God confidently, knowing He is faithful in responding to my petitions.

> Have you ever prayed to God, and you did get an answer? What did you do?

REFLECT

_____

_____

_____

_____

_____

YOUR PERSONAL PRAYER

_____

_____

_____

_____

_____

_____

_____

_____

_____

1 Samuel 2:2 (NIV): "There is no one holy like the Lord; there is no one besides you; there is no Rock like our God."

Holies are you, Lord

Out of the sanctuary, worship came.
Giving thanks unto God to whom all praises belong.
He whose heavenly angels sing holy, holy are you, Lord.
To the one who is and is to come.
Every hidden part of me cries out holy are you, Lord.
Oh, restful thought, you can cry out.
With the sweetness of harmonica and piano lines.
Joyous mouths to Him they sing.
A bed of love-tuning harmony rings out.
cries out holy are you, Lord.
A breathless voice struggles to stay alive.
Hoping for a spirit-filled life
Filled with his love,
A joyous love to witness
A joyous communion with the Lord.
Awaiting the Lord, who is holy to come.

As a child of God, I believe it is essential to show reverence to Him. Acknowledging His holiness, uniqueness, purity, and supreme majesty is central to my faith and daily life. It reminds me of His greatness and my responsibility to honor Him in everything I do

> Have you ever wondered about the Holy of Holies? What does it mean to encounter God's presence in your life?

REFLECT

_____

_____

_____

_____

_____

_____

YOUR PERSONAL PRAYER

_____

_____

_____

_____

_____

_____

_____

_____

_____

_____

Isaiah 25:4 (NIV) - "You have been a refuge for the poor, a refuge for the needy in their distress, a shelter from the storm and a shade from the heat. For the breath of the ruthless is like a storm driving against a wall."

Protective shade

I search for that protective shade.
Looking beyond the clouds.
As I observe the sun going down.
Looking at the bold, brilliant, and rich colors
Sinking into the calmest of the night to be.
Hoping for one, just to delight to sit in his shade.
My heart quickened my soul came alive.
when the magical colors blinded my eyes.
Holding steadfast just to see
Waiting in awe for my light to shine.
The covering I seek the protective shade I know.
Will protect me no matter where I go.
My shelter from the storm, my need to only depend on Him.
I accept his offering as my shade and sanctuary.
Relying on God to provide my refuge.
Knowing that he is my shelter and my protector.
Like refreshing water that cannot dry up.

I believe God is our protector; He is the protector of my soul and the security guard of my spirit. Psalms 121:5 reads, "The Lord watches over you; the Lord is your shade at your right hand." I trust that He offers me shade and refuge from the challenges and trials of my life.

Have you ever turned your heart to God thanking him for the? shelter he provides for you.

REFLECT

_____

_____

_____

_____

_____

YOUR PERSONAL PRAYER

_____

_____

_____

_____

_____

_____

_____

_____

Isaiah 58:11 (NIV) - "The Lord will guide you always; he will satisfy your needs in a sun-scorched land and will strengthen your frame. You will be like a well-watered garden, like a spring whose waters never fail."

Bubbling up of Spring water of life

Oh, look at the Spring, it is silent.
Oh, look at the water sitting like it has no life.
Spring, oh Spring brings life to me.
What lies beneath you oh Spring.
Is it well that I can thirst no more?
Withdrawing from the scriptures that are kept in my heart.
Satisfying a longing that continues to grow.
Oh, Spring can I come and drink?
Anticipating that the Spirit of God will purify the water.
I heard Spring has everlasting water, and I will thirst no more.
Will I have eternal life, oh bubbling Spring come back, come back.
Bring the refreshments I seek, regeneration I must.
Hoping for sustenance that spring water will give everlasting life.

I see God's Spirit's abundant and life-giving nature as a river or spring of living water that brings refreshment, renewal, and spiritual nourishment to my life. It springs forth, symbolizing spiritual renewal, abundance, and eternal life, reminding me of His unending grace and sustenance.

How does the imagery of a "bubbling spring" means to you personally regarding to God's grace and love?

REFLECT

_____

_____

_____

_____

_____

YOUR PERSONAL PRAYER

_____

_____

_____

_____

_____

_____

_____

_____

_____

1 John 5:14 (NIV) - "This is the confidence we have in approaching God: that if we ask anything according to his will, he hears us."

If only I can listen

If only I could listen oh Lord
If only I could hear from you O Lord.
If only my intentions can determine the outcome
If only my cry can be heard
If only you could see or hear me oh Lord
I listened to hear from you oh Lord.
I sit for days, hours, months, and years just to hear from you O Lord.
My prayers seem to be in a vapor.
Waiting in silence for God to speak.
Believing in his promise according to his will.
Then suddenly I looked up and heard your whisper.
Saying come, sit, Stop, and listen to hear my voice.
He says I will always listen to you.
O God may I listen, my ear incline to hear you.
Speak Lord, your voice I hear.
Sending me to where I should go.

These verses express my desire for God to search, know, and examine my innermost thoughts, intentions, and desires. They reflect my prayerful attitude of openness and surrendering before Him, inviting His scrutiny and guidance in leading a righteous life.

> Ask God, for the spirit of discernment so that you can hear from Him.

REFLECT

_____

_____

_____

_____

_____

YOUR PERSONAL PRAYER

_____

_____

_____

_____

_____

_____

_____

_____

_____

Psalm 25:4-5 (NIV): "Show me your ways, Lord, teach me your paths. Guide me in your truth and teach me, for you are God my Savior, and my hope is in you all day long."

Teach me

Teach me my heavenly father how to sing.
Open my mouth so that the praises can ring.
Let me learn how to ask for your blessings.
So that I can walk into my destiny.

Teach me Heavenly Father how to feel restless.
So that I can sit and listen to your call.
Waiting for the time to come.
So that my heart and mind can become.

Then I will be inspired knowing that your
hand will guide me all the way.
To teach me about the words to say.
Upon my desk for all to see.
Awaken their souls for them to see.

Oh, how I learned how to discern right from wrong.
To trust only you, my Lord.
I will wait for you to direct my path.
Even when the path is dark, and everything seems hopeless.
Your teaching always find a way.

As a believer in Christ, I personally learned how to listen to hear the voice of God. During my time of reflection and stillness, I realize that the Holy Spirit teaches me and opens my mind and heart. When I need to understand the spiritual truths found in the Bible, I trust the Holy Spirit to guide me. God's word inspires me, teaches me what is true, shows me what is wrong, corrects me, and teaches me what is right.

> Have you ever asked God what is missing so that you can boldly praise Him wholeheartedly?

REFLECT

_____

_____

_____

_____

_____

YOUR PERSONAL PRAYER

_____

_____

_____

_____

_____

_____

_____

_____

_____

Isaiah 40:31 (NIV): "But those who hope in the Lord will renew their strength. They will soar on wings like eagles; they will run and not grow weary; they will walk and not faint."

God prepares you for the journey

Prepare me oh God for the journey of life.
young, foolish anxious are my thoughts.
Hope was never too far off
Faith was just around the corner.
Lurking to see if my way is clear.
Just look my Lord the journey has just begun.
I am waiting for your hands to lead me along the way.
I am waiting for your guidance.
This journey is full of obstacles along the way.
I know my journey will not be in vain.
I know my preparation will not be lost.
I know my father God will be there every step of the way.
Journeying along with faith, as hopes arises, and peace begins.
Just to hear His voice saying, walk with me don't be afraid.

My life is a journey with God filled with gratitude, thanksgiving, and praise. From a young age, my grandmother taught me to be thankful for every blessing. As I grew older, my dependence on God deepened, guiding me through seasons of growth, change, and steadfast faith. Even when the path is hard to predict, I know that God's comforting presence remains constant in moments of sorrow, despair, and fear.

> How can you align your purpose with the plan of God and how can you find strength and guidance for the journey he has prepare for you?

REFLECT

_____

_____

_____

_____

_____

YOUR PERSONAL PRAYER

_____

_____

_____

_____

_____

_____

_____

_____

Philippians 4:6-7 (NIV): "Do not be anxious about anything, but in every situation, by prayer and petition, with thanksgiving, present your requests to God. And the peace of God, which transcends all understanding, will guard your hearts and your minds in Christ Jesus."

The Raging Storm Within

The storm is raging, when will it stop?
The storm of trouble is twirling around me when will peace comes.
Where can I hide, where can I hurry to find Thee?
The temper of the storm rages.
I feel afraid, I feel lost.
Then I cried out to the Lord
He still the storm to a whisper.
And stop the raging sea to a hushed.
He provided a resting place.
He found shelter and shade for me.
He removes the dark clouds.
He opens the sun to shine on me.
My fear vanishes, my hope restored.
The rainbow of hope hovers above.
With the sunshine of mercy and a joyful heart.
The storm is over, and the shadows are gone.

In life's storms, God provides comfort and encouragement. When I was in a seemingly hopeless situation, He sent caring individuals and a supportive church community to uplift me. Even while suffering, He strengthens and consoles me. I can testify to this truth: no matter what trials come my way, if I continue to trust Him, He will never leave my side, walking with me through every step of the journey.

Have you ever thought what is the purpose of the storm raging within you? Reflect on how you can find peace with God for a better outcome.

REFLECT

_____

_____

_____

_____

_____

YOUR PERSONAL PRAYER

_____

_____

_____

_____

_____

_____

_____

_____

_____

_____

Isaiah 40:29 (NIV): "He gives strength to the weary and increases the power of the weak."

Just a woman

Some say I am just a woman; she can bear the pain.
Others say she is strong, she needs no help.
Strength and honor are her clothing.
What more could she want?
In her Laugh with distress; she feels the pain.
She stumbled in hope, integrity is her strength.
Her happiness becomes her treasure.
As she opens her mouth and wisdom leaves.
They say she works with a willing hand.
Others say she teaches with kindness and love.
She prays that her children are in God's handiwork.
What more does she want?
She fears the Lord, and she knows him.
She said, He should be praised always.
She is always in Control of her emotions.
Even when she is breaking.
She knows that she is just a woman.
Who is weak indeed?
Who needs rest from the battles of life?
Knowing that her God is in control.

During my years as a single parent, I often felt consumed by fatigue and exhaustion. Yet, my only refuge was turning to God. Those moments felt like a nightmare I wanted to forget, but His grace rescued me repeatedly. Each year, I reflect, whisper prayers, and allow Him to shape my heart. I discovered that proper rest is found when I draw near God.

As a struggling woman, how can you ask for guidance, wisdom and understanding in your struggles that will bring compassion grounded in humility and trust that only can come from Jesus Christ

REFLECT

_____

_____

_____

_____

_____

YOUR PERSONAL PRAYER

_____

_____

_____

_____

_____

_____

_____

_____

_____

Psalm 34:18 (NIV): "The Lord is close to the brokenhearted and saves those who are crushed in spirit.

The pain within

The pain within is hard to bear.
The pain within me is speaking to me.
The pain within me is calling to my heart.
The pain within me needs time to communicate.
The pain is starting to heat up like a furnace.
Hoping for someone to cool it.
God is blowing his breath upon my pain.
A cooling that will bring relief.
A pain that needs to surrender.
Trembling, I am frightened I cannot go on living.
My words or groaning can express the aches of my pain.
I need to know you are there.
To be my refuge from my pain.
To replace my distress with peace.
And your strength with my weakness.
I do not understand dear Lord.
But my trust and comfort lie in you.
As I grow faint, I hear God is calling.
Wait, I only can take your pain away.

Before I had my knee surgery, the pain was excruciating, something I wouldn't wish upon anyone. It was chronic, frustrating, and disrupted my daily activities. My breathing quickened, as stressful hormones surged through my body. Although medication provided temporary relief, what indeed carried me through my most challenging moments was the knowledge that God was with me. I trusted in His presence, love, and promise of ultimate restoration. That hope and comfort reminded me I was never alone in my suffering.

During your suffering there is confusion, and you feel overwhelmed sometimes forgetting God. Do you ever feel excruciating pain that your wounder where is your God?

REFLECT

_____

_____

_____

_____

_____

_____

YOUR PERSONAL PRAYER

_____

_____

_____

_____

_____

_____

_____

_____

_____

Psalm 37:7 says "Be still before the LORD and wait patiently for him; do not fret when people succeed in their ways when they carry out their wicked schemes".

Patience

How can I wait for patience to come?
Patience is saying hold on I will be right there.
Patience says you can wait.
But I am telling you I cannot wait.
I cannot hope, no more.
Wishing for you and wondering when.
Patience says look as far as you can see,
I am coming says patience.
It is not my time.
Stay focused, keep believing I am coming.
Patience answered to wait,
My time is not your time.
I do not see the time I see faith.
I sit in confusion; I am feeling uncomfortable with what you said.
My mind keeps wandering because patience
is taking too much time to come.
Then patience said, do you not know.
God is patience, he always keeps his promise.

Waiting on God does not mean I am inactive. I learned from an early age that waiting means trusting faithfully and obeying Him. Sometimes, I am so caught up in my own ways and what I want that I miss what God is doing in me rather than embracing the growth in waiting on Him.

When you engage in a dialogue with Jesus about patience It will help you to understand and fully trust him. Ask God to help you to cultivate patience in your daily life.

REFLECT

_____

_____

_____

_____

_____

_____

YOUR PERSONAL PRAYER

_____

_____

_____

_____

_____

_____

_____

_____

_____

_____

John 3: KJV: The wind bloweth where it listeth, and thou hearest the sound thereof, but canst not tell whence it cometh, and whither it goeth: so is every one that is born of the Spirit.

God's Winds

The wind blows wherever it goes.
It blows the leaves near and far.
The tender leaves are too tired to rest.
The leaves Cry out Father give us some rest.
Gods said the wind is there to teach you.
The wind is there to guide you home.
Oh, tree do not be scared.
You are stronger than you appear.
My wind is there to blow away your sorrow.
The storm is there to shake your branches.
The wind can beat, shake, and sometimes break you.
Through every tempest, you will stand.
The strong roots that you planted will stay anchored.
Grounded for everyone to see.
God's north wind rides upon the clouds and brings hope for everyone.
With blessings and joy upon his mighty wings.

I also think about the wind. I can't see it, yet I feel it around me. Similarly, I cannot see God but sense His presence. Sometimes, He speaks to me through a gentle breeze, reminding me of His nearness. Perhaps the same is true of the Holy Spirit—ever present and always at work, even though I don't physically see Him.

> **Have you ever observed the wind blowing within the leaves? What are your thoughts?**

REFLECT

_____

_____

_____

_____

_____

_____

YOUR PERSONAL PRAYER

_____

_____

_____

_____

_____

_____

_____

_____

_____

_____

2nd Corinthians 4:6 (NIV): "For God, who said, 'Let light shine out of darkness,' made his light shine in our hearts to give us the light of the knowledge of God's glory displayed in the face of Christ".

The brightness of God

The soft sweet honey dripping from the tree sac is delicious to eat.
As the splendid summers exemplifies his beauty to behold.
The beautiful flowers grew in splendor.
Bright is his glory, bright for all to see.
Bright are his seasons, the lighted days shows his splendor.
As the sun looks down upon its brightness.
Worshiping to his God that makes all things bright.
The moonlight he gives to guide me on my way.
His brightness is not to take too likely.
His brightness brings hope, his brightness brings joy.
God's brightness is all I need.
A brightness that cannot be outshined.
That brings heartfelt joy that will cover you and me.

When I think about physical light, I recognize how it helps me see in the dark, enabling me to navigate when I would otherwise be lost. Similarly, I believe God's light, revealed through the Bible, reflects His glory. I also think this divine light shines within me so I can share it with others, illuminating their path and reflecting God's love in the world.

The brightness of Jesus signifies spiritual guidance and hope for humanity. How can His brightness replicate your light in your daily interaction with others?

REFLECT

_____

_____

_____

_____

_____

_____

YOUR PERSONAL PRAYER

_____

_____

_____

_____

_____

_____

_____

_____

_____

_____

Isaiah 42:3 He will not crush the weakest reed or put out a flickering candle. He will bring justice to all who have been wronged.

Light me Lord like a candle

The candlelight flickers and the candlelight dims.
The candlelight flickers and fights to stay alive.
How O Lord will you keep my light lit like the candlelight?
How O Lord can my strength not flicker?
How O Lord will my frame not swayed when trouble arrives?
How O Lord can I stay my course when my enemies triumph over me
I know Lord, I know Lord.
The candlelight of Jesus shines in my presence
The light that shines so brightly for me to see.
All the darkness will disappear.
Jesus' candlelight directs me along the path.
A path that was dark so that I could not see.
Bringing me out of that darkness.
Walking into a new world that is filled with light and hope.
Shining brightly for all to see.
A light shining far off sending hope to someone.
As the light draws closer, his presence brings favor.
Opening a path for everyone to see
Recognizing that Jesus' light is the candlelight.

As I watched the gentle flicker of a candle, I reflected on how fragile my life can sometimes feel—just like that tiny flame. Yet, I trust that God doesn't snuff me out; He lovingly nurtures and sustains me. This realization reminds me to lean on Him when I'm at my weakest, finding comfort and strength in His enduring compassion.

Do you think that God will extinguish you when you are in your vulnerable state?

REFLECT

_____

_____

_____

_____

_____

YOUR PERSONAL PRAYER

_____

_____

_____

_____

_____

_____

_____

_____

_____

Hebrews 4:13 (NIV): "Nothing in all creation is hidden from God's sight. Everything is uncovered and laid bare before the eyes of him to whom we must give account

Whose eyes are you seeing Through?

I am looking for the eyes of God.
Eyes that I can follow.
A lens that is so bright to see.
Taking me to his will.
As I pray daily to see what he sees.
As I ran away from the darkness
Lord, you said do not be afraid, do not run.
There is no darkness in your eyes.
Look Open Your Eyes the sun is shining brightly.
See my eyes are looking, not searching because I see you.
My eyes are there, looking for your eyes.
Showing an abundance of love that is freely given.
Worthy of the new beginnings that He gives.
A bible that gives my viewpoint about your life.
For my eyes are upon you, guiding you to your destiny.

As I reflect on Jesus Christ and how He walked this earth doing good to everyone, I try to follow His example. By offering a simple smile, holding an elderly person's hand as they cross the street, or sharing a warm cup of coffee, I'm reminded of how a small act of kindness can brighten someone's day. In these moments, I see the world through Jesus's eyes.

Looking through God's eyes means seeking his perspective in our daily lives. Pray to God to give you the ability through prayers and open your eyes to see situations and people from his point of view.

REFLECT

YOUR PERSONAL PRAYER

Psalm 91:1 (NIV): "Whoever dwells in the shelter of the highest will rest in the shadow of the Almighty."

In the hidden place

There is a hidden place.
That no one can see.
Is where God visits you daily.
It is your time you spend with God.
It is a home you seek for your refuge.
As I pushed through each morning waiting for him to arrive.
Just to say good morning
Just to feel his presence
Just to get a quickening from his spirit to read his word.
In that hidden place, I know I am love.
In that hidden place, I know I am fed.
In that hidden place, I know my joy is fulfilled.
In that hidden place, God's will words rang out.
Saying I will be secure in his embrace.
My laughter will be heard, the battle is won.
In that hidden place, no one sees.
There God's love will be revealed.
An incomparable love cannot be measured.
because it was given in a hidden place.

In God's hidden place, I find peace, love, comfort, protection, and refuge as I seek Him. I have my secret place where I seek God's presence daily. Each day, I ask God to separate me from the things that do not give Him glory, allowing me to focus on His will and purpose for my life.

As we reflect on our hidden place where we can go and seek God's presence, consider asking God how can you experience his presence so that you can experience or find the peace he offers.

REFLECT

_____

_____

_____

_____

_____

YOUR PERSONAL PRAYER

_____

_____

_____

_____

_____

_____

_____

_____

_____

_____

Isaiah 30:21 (NIV): "Whether you turn to the right or the left, your ears will hear a voice behind you, saying, 'This is the way; walk in it.'"

Hear his voice

Hear his voice when he responds to my cry.
I hear his voice when he is calling my name.
His voice sings when hardship presents itself.
His voice opened his heart to hear when I speak.
I hear his voice when he embraces me.
I heard his voice when I needed correction, direction, and guidance.
Yes, I heard his voice when I was delivered.
I heard his voice when the wind blew.
As I look at the trees.
I heard his voice when the earth shook, as he displayed his handiworks.
Commanding everyone to stand in his presence.
A holy voice that thundered throughout the skies.
Waiting for his people to gather at attention.
I believe in his voice, always listening with open ears.
Oh yes, I know that is his voice because he knows my voice.

Jesus has been calling me to listen to His voice. As I move about my day, I ask God to help me stay focused on Him and keep me obedient to His calling. I know that God speaks to me through the Holy Spirit, and I need to remain in His presence to hear Him clearly and follow His guidance.

God can communicate with us in many ways. It may be audible, it can manifest through our thoughts, feelings, circumstance or through others via counselling. Ask God how can you cultivate listening habits and become attuned to the subtle cues that he is sending to you.

REFLECT

_____

_____

_____

_____

_____

YOUR PERSONAL PRAYER

_____

_____

_____

_____

_____

_____

_____

_____

_____

Luke 12:35-36 (NIV): "Be dressed ready for service and keep your lamps burning, like servants waiting for their master to return from a wedding banquet so that when he comes and knocks, they can immediately open the door for him."

Gather your things

I was told to gather my things.
I was told to hurry because I must leave.
I was told to watch do not go to sleep.
I was told to answer the call when the bell rang.
I know that I must be ready.
I know that I must not tarry.
I know that he is calling.
I know my destiny awaits.
I know that my answer is in the gathering.
I know that I must obey.
I know that abundance overflow awaits.
I know that I must follow his calling.
I know that he awaits as I gather my things.
Trusting and seeking wisdom so that I can tackle what awaits ahead.

This poem captures my heartfelt questions to God about why my desire takes so long to manifest. It weighs heavily on my heart, especially as I feel a growing urgency with time passing and no visible progress. Waiting often feels like a test of endurance and faith. In those moments, I wrestle with impatience, discouragement, worry, and doubts about God's care. Yet, I hold firmly to the truth that Christ never wastes waiting time. He uses it to refine, shape, and strengthen me for His purpose.

Have you ever considered writing down what your soul needs to seek divine guidance for your own spiritual focus. Gathering your things symbolize seeking God and trusting that when he comes you will be ready for Him.

REFLECT

YOUR PERSONAL PRAYER

John 6:35 (NIV): "Then Jesus declared, 'I am the bread of life. Whoever comes to me will never go hungry, and whoever believes in me will never be thirsty."

My living food

I look beyond my garden trying to find my food.
I searched within the surrounding fields for my food.
I walk by the river trying to find my food.
I look far over the mountains.
just to see if the food is there.
I am desperate to eat from the food I have heard about.
I cried to El Rohi, and he heard my cry.
A cry that my father heard.
My eyes are looking all over.
I need that food, which will take away my hunger.
He said come, my daughter,
I will feed you,
I will not let you hunger anymore.
I am the food you are looking for.
A food that you will never be hungry.

Jesus declares, "Whoever comes to me will never go hungry." These words ignite a deep longing within me for God's desire to have the right relationship with Him. I must hunger and thirst for God's word and passionately seek to be in His presence, as it is there that I find true fulfillment and peace.

This poem resonates a deep sincere longing for Jesus. Tell him you are not seeking physical substance but to have a spiritual relationship with Him. Consider asking Jesus for the food He gives, not only for earthly needs but for your eternal soul.

REFLECT

_____

_____

_____

_____

_____

_____

YOUR PERSONAL PRAYER

_____

_____

_____

_____

_____

_____

_____

_____

_____

Isiah 43:19 (NIV): "See, I am doing a new thing! Now it springs up; do you not perceive it? I am making a way in the wilderness and streams in the wasteland."

It is never too late to be his presence

The Lord says is never too late.
to cross over the river.
A river that is flowing despite the problems and obstacles that I face.
But when the river seemed to stop, you said to come.
It is never too late for something new.
I am the beginning and the end.
Come and if you fall, I will wait for you.
If you stop to pick up someone, I will wait.
Time is not my problem.
Coming and entering my presence.
It is never too late.
Enter my door, I will keep it open for you.
Do not look back; stay focused.
I am here to help you. When I am in your presence.
It is never too late for you to meet with your Lord.
Come there is peace within my presence.
It is never to late for you to call on me.

It's never too late to turn to God for His protection and guidance. By seeking God's presence daily and trusting Him, I trust He will lead me on the right path to righteousness. It may not always be easy, but I find peace and clarity when I am in His presence.

It is never too late to be in the presence of God. No matter the circumstances, the trials and disappointments you faced it is never too late. Reflect more on how you can draw near to Him. You can always seek Him; his presence is always available no matter what time.

REFLECT

_____

_____

_____

_____

_____

_____

YOUR PERSONAL PRAYER

_____

_____

_____

_____

_____

_____

_____

_____

_____

1ST Corinthians 1:18 (NIV): "For the message of the cross is foolishness to those who are perishing, but to us who are being saved it is the power of God."

The cross is my altar

He died on the cross for me.
He bleeds on the tree for me.
He knows what rejection feels like for me.
He knows what alienation feels like.
He came to me, and I knew him not.
I did not honor him.
His blood has been given to me for royalty.
Because he did not hold back anything.
I deviated from his laws.
I deviated from his commandments.
I deviated from his Kingdom.
I deviated from his statutes.
I chose to disobey him.
His blood supersedes all his laws.
Just to save me.
Oh, how can I find grace and not destroy me?
Oh, how can I find my Lord?
Oh, I cannot make this opportunity run out.
The structure of my life depends on the cross.
The cross that carries me day by day.

When I say the cross is my altar, I mean that what Jesus has done for me is the cornerstone of my faith and life. It is where I discover my true purpose and identity. By declaring this, I acknowledge Jesus's profound role in my life through His ultimate sacrifice, reconciling me with the Father and giving me hope.

In what way can you say the cross is your Altar. Do you reflect on how Jesus offered Himself as the final and perfect sacrifice for us.

REFLECT

_____

_____

_____

_____

_____

YOUR PERSONAL PRAYER

_____

_____

_____

_____

_____

_____

_____

_____

_____

Psalm 107:28-29 "Then they cried out to the Lord in their trouble, and he brought them out of their distress. He stilled the storm to a whisper; the waves of the sea were hushed".

My Life is a Reflection of the Ocean

Sometimes I am calm.
Sometimes I get rage inside.
What am I, who am I, and where am I?
I look at my calmness and I see the Ocean.
I look at my rage or anger and I see the Ocean.
My life reflects both.
Sometimes it seems like the Ocean is crying out to God,
As I also cry out to Him.
The Ocean is God's creation.
I am God's creation.
The Ocean is good and full of life, and so am I.
It does not speak but it shows its feelings.
The waves show their rage at times.
But calmest becomes its peace.
The Ocean feeds, it cleanses,
It swallows and spits things out.
Waiting to be clean again as it looks around.
When the ocean sees the visitor coming, it leaps with joy.
Dancing as life creates, experiencing God's glory.
No one knows where it begin or end.
His reflection of its calmness brings me harmony.
Knowing that the One who create us, can bring us rest.
A rest that is needed as we flow.

When I gaze at the ocean, I see a reflection of my journey—vast, mysterious, and full of unknowns. The waves remind me of the rhythms of my life. Some days bring gentle, calming moments, while others surge with intensity and challenge. My emotions rise and fall like tides; sometimes, I wrestle with anger, and at other times, I find serenity. Yet, I am reminded that God created the ocean with intention and beauty and made me with a unique purpose. Every wave, every storm, and every calm are part of His perfect plan for my life, flowing into His more incredible design.

We must learn to embrace the powerful and calm waves of our lives and recognized that God is with us always. How do you feel about the ocean, is there any specific aspect of the ocean that resonates most with you regarding your life.

REFLECT

_____

_____

_____

_____

YOUR PERSONAL PRAYER

_____

_____

_____

_____

_____

Proverbs 4:23, "Above all else, guard your heart, for everything you do flows from it."

Streams of Living Water

Oh river, where will you flow?
Will it be downstream, or will it be upstream?
The dry patch of land is thirsty.
Awaiting your arrival.
People of God stand, waiting for you.
oh water, how ironic that the water stands like a tree.
Not moving in the dry patchy place.
watching, and waiting for its time to flow.
Waiting for him to come.
The water is waiting to hear his voice.
Waiting for the right time to flow.
Then the water starts flowing for all eyes to see.
All ears to hear.
Flowing, arising as the wind directs.
Trusting that the water will bring.
An outpouring of his spirit for you to see.
A heart that is waiting for the overflow.

Sometimes, I feel an unexplainable dryness, a deep longing for something to satisfy an indescribable thirst. But as I seek God's presence, I realize He uses these moments to prepare my heart to rely entirely on Him. Though these seasons can be challenging, they also bring comfort, reminding me that God is shaping my faith and teaching me to trust Him completely.

Have you ever thirsted for the streams of living water in your life? Reflect on how Jesus who is the "Living Water" can quench your thirst and fulfill your life with a fullness you cannot comprehend.

REFLECT

_____

_____

_____

_____

_____

YOUR PERSONAL PRAYER

_____

_____

_____

_____

_____

_____

_____

_____

_____

Isaiah 26:3, NIV: You will keep in perfect peace, those whose minds are steadfast, because they trust in you.

Silence My Negative Thoughts

I heard the voices of people roaming all around me.
My thoughts are listening to the one who tells it all.
As I listened the voices seemed to grow heavier and stronger.
On the part, I dread to go.
My thoughts are stressful and need a pause.
Come, do not disturb my thoughts.
It is on a transformational journey.
Renewing new ideas of wholeness.
Oh, negative thoughts, I cannot hear,
The trauma, my experience, my woundedness,
and the opinions of others.
My negative thoughts are changing. My
negative thoughts are developing.
Look up negative mind, look up negative thoughts.
You cannot attack me anymore.
His strength, his love, and his peace are coming.
Teaching, growing, and developing me.
Into the person Christ desires, me to be,
My deliverer is here to set my mind free.
The battle will be won.

As a child of God, I know how vital it is to renew my mind daily by replacing negative thoughts with the truth found in His Word. When I bring God's knowledge into my situations, His truth transforms my perspective. I can overcome negativity and gain clarity by spending consistent time in His presence. I rely on the guidance in His Word to fight and win the battles within my mind.

How have you dealt with your negative anxious and doubtful thoughts that have been consuming your mind. Share how you dealt with your thoughts.

REFLECT

_____

_____

_____

_____

_____

YOUR PERSONAL PRAYER

_____

_____

_____

_____

_____

_____

_____

_____

_____

Matthew 6:22 says, "The eye is the lamp of the body. If your eyes are good, your whole body will be full of light. But if your eye is bad, your whole body will be full of darkness. If therefore the light that is in you is darkness, how great is that darkness?

My eyes see the sorrows of my soul

Open my eyes oh Lord so that I can see my soul.
Oh, soul that holds so much sadness, only my eyes can see,
open my eyes, behold my eyes know the truth.
It knows the darkest part of my soul.
It can bring light in the darkness.
A brighter light that is so bright.
Bedazzle the sorrows of my soul.
I see my eyes looking through my heart.
Trying to clean up the mess that was caused.
To set my soul free again.
Oh, eyes search for my freedom.
so that I can be set free.
The soul needs to be replenished.
Before the enemies come to be destroyed.
Oh, the soul keeps glancing up at the eyes.
Oh, yes what do you see: A God that notices my soul.
Eyes that are dazzled as the stars in the sky.
A soul that beholds the beautiful light.
Remove the sorrow from my heart.
Oh, soul you are connected to my eyes.
Eyes can take the message to the light,

Our eyes reveal so much—they reflect pain, grief, sorrows, and joys. But what if we used our eyes to tell God's story? When someone looks into my eyes, I want them to see the love of God shining through. As a part of who I am, my eyes hold the power to hide or reveal my emotions. I pray that I will always reflect on His light, to share love, and grace with everyone I meet.

Your eyes see the pain and sadness and turmoil you are experiencing. Your eyes see your soul's sorrow. What sorrow are you feeling right now that you need God to guide you.

REFLECT

_____

_____

_____

_____

_____

_____

YOUR PERSONAL PRAYER

_____

_____

_____

_____

_____

_____

Psalm 139:23 says, "Search me, O God, and know my heart; try me and know my thoughts".

The Soil Metaphor of my soul

My soul is like the dry soil.
In dry parched land.
Dry soil that needs water because it is thirsty.
A soul that needs to survive.
Gazing at the dry parch land.
Watching the soil drinking it all up.
My soul is crying out to God to give me the water.
My soil holds so many memories, thoughts, and hopes.
Hold on my soul, do not give up.
My testimony, my flaws are in you.
Hold on to Jesus for His water will never run dry.
He can refresh and fertilize, my soul.
Oh, earth I see you as a metaphor for me.
Praying for the living water to come.
To quench my soul, to break the chains.
So that I can glean from the soil waiting
for a seed to burst from the soil.

I sometimes feel spiritually dry, like a parched earth longing for rain. Yet, I hold onto the truth that after the rain falls, the earth softens, and new life begins to grow. This reminds me that renewal will come in God's perfect time, and it keeps me from relying on my feelings alone.

When experiencing spiritual dryness, ask God questions like what is causing it. Seek His help in understanding your emotions and trusting Him beyond how you feel.

REFLECT

YOUR PERSONAL PRAYER

Psalm 90:17 "Let the favor of the Lord our God be upon us and establish the work of our hands upon us; yes, establish the work of our hands!"

My favor

Have mercy on me oh Lord.
So that my gates may be opened.
You will provide the key that will open the padlock door.
Waiting for my inheritance.
Your favor will extend to me.
Your glory O, Lord will anoint me.
Your favor or Lord will be remembered.
Upon my generation and generations to come
Oh, Lord come and visit me.
Look and see how your benefits are holding me up for all to see.
For no one can be compared to you.
For your favor is from everlasting to everlasting.
For your favor over me cannot be compared
To a flood of water washing away my impurities.
Arise God send your favor.
Against the enemies that surround me.
Each one falls as they go.
Because grace is your unmerited favor.
And blessing becomes my overflow.

Walking in God's favor is a daily choice I commit to wholeheartedly. While it's not always easy, I believe the first step is transforming my mind and aligning my thoughts with His Word. God's favor can open unimaginable doors, create extraordinary opportunities, and connect me with people I never envisioned meeting. By faithfully following Jesus, I trust He will equip me with everything I need to walk confidently along the path He has designed for me.

Finding favor with God is not about been perfect or trying to earn his love. God wants us to be obedient and align our life with his will. What are some of the things you can do that will reflect the way Jesus wants us to live.

REFLECT

_____

_____

_____

_____

_____

YOUR PERSONAL PRAYER

_____

_____

_____

_____

_____

_____

_____

_____

_____

John 16:13: "But when he, the Spirit of truth, comes, he will guide you into all the truth. He will not speak on his own; he will speak only what he hears, and he will tell you what is yet to come."

Spiritual compass

Where are you leading me?
Where is the place God is sending me?
As I watch the internal compass.
I wonder what direction I must go.
I prayed but it did not lead me there.
How must I pray oh, spiritual compass?
Should I fast or should I pray?
Just to guide the compass to where I should go.
Should I become aware of the dangers that I cannot see ahead?
Awaken my spiritual compass.
I need to find my path.
To serve God, so that my spiritual part can stay on track.
No idols and no circles can hold me back.
Because God's spiritual compass can lead the way.
Activate, so that I can go on my journey.
To seek hope, joy, and peace.
To worship God as He directs the rudder towards my part.

The Holy Spirit serves as God's spiritual compass, guiding my decisions and the paths I take. It leads me through the uncharted territories of my life, helping me navigate challenges and overcome obstacles. Likewise, the Bible is my Map, offering divine revelation and clarity about my direction. As a child of God, I am blessed with the freedom of choice, allowing me to move freely while staying rooted in His love and purpose for my life.

What specific areas in your life that you are asking God to send his spiritual compass to help you to navigate your journey with confidence and to stay on the path He wants you to go.

REFLECT

_____

_____

_____

_____

_____

YOUR PERSONAL PRAYER

_____

_____

_____

_____

_____

_____

_____

_____

_____

1st Corinthians 2:9 "Eye has not seen, nor ear heard, nor have entered into the heart of man, the things which God has prepared for those who love Him.

Flood manifestation

Springs of sweet water.
Bring in the flood to revive my soul.
The garden that I keep watering is the source of my glory.
That I the Lord can come and interrupt your life.
I heard a small voice saying I called you to be a flood.
So that everyone can wash and be cleanse to enter my Kingdom.
To manifest my glory, oh come let us celebrate.
I will give you my blessings.
A flooding of blessing you cannot understand.
Showing goodness mercy and compassion to all.
so that you may have an everlasting overflow.
Overflowing in every good works.
beginning in Jesus grace and mercy.
That will over fill with a flooding of love.
So that we can share the water with the world.
To manifest His glory for all to see.

I thank God, my Father, for the abundance and overflow He is pouring into my life. Through this overflow, I can bless others and guide them toward discovering the rich spiritual abundance God has in store for them. Together, we can share His blessings and pour His love and grace into the lives of many.

Can you imagine seeing a powerful outpouring of God's presence, God's favor can manifest .as a flood in your life. Are you willing to trust God that He can bring into your life an overflow of flood manifestation. How can you surrender to God the areas in your life that you are lacking in.

REFLECT

_____

_____

_____

_____

_____

YOUR PERSONAL PRAYER

_____

_____

_____

_____

_____

_____

_____

_____

James 4:7-8a (NIV): "Submit yourselves, then, to God. Resist the devil, and he will flee from you. Come near to God and he will come near to you."

What shall I surrender ?

I internalize my feelings and my heart bears the burden.
Oh, God, I need fresh measurements to measure myself.
My past failures, my jealousy, my hurdles, my relationship,
All these personality needs to surrender to you.
Oh God, my reactions are emotional.
All these reaction is coming from where I have been.
where I came from.
Oh God, please come, help me.
Break the wall down inside of me.
Sometimes God it is the smallest things I hold in my heart.
Clean my heart, let go of things, and I must seek repentance.
Pride stands in my way; arrogance stands in my way.
Take them Jesus, take it all.
As I humbly seek your guidance and ask for direction.
From a mess, up heart that must be healed.
Surrendering all I have, at your feet Jesus.

Trusting in God is a profound surrender, requiring faith to believe that Jesus can deliver, even in uncertainty. I surrender every part of myself and everything I hold to God. By letting go of control and inviting Him in, I embrace the truth that His ways are higher, His thoughts are more remarkable, and His plans far exceed mine.

Ask God what are you holding on to that is holding you back to totally surrender to him? Are there any areas of your life that you find hard to surrender.

REFLECT

_____

_____

_____

_____

_____

YOUR PERSONAL PRAYER

_____

_____

_____

_____

_____

_____

_____

_____

Ephesians 2:10 reads, "For we are his workmanship, created in Christ Jesus unto good works, which God hath before ordained that we should walk in them."

Birthing A new me

The vision of birth is rising within me.
Songs of love are knocking at my door.
I see my habits are changing.
I see my change attitude will impact my life.
Only to glorify you.
I can see the outcome of spending time with you.
Gives me Confidence to step out.
I am no longer afraid.
My thoughts symbolize new beginnings.
My heart is rejoicing.
A new life is being born within me.
Lord prepares me for what is destined for me.
Watch out! disappointments, rejection, trauma, failures.
I can see your plan now.
The lost parts are in the hidden desires.
Bring them back to life for me.
A new me is born.
Embracing change from the inside out.
Sending an overflow of his spirit.
To become my companion and guide me into a new person.

The first work of grace begins when God starts working in my heart. Trusting in Him can transform sadness, pain, trauma, and disappointments. His grace can bring renewal, healing, and new outcomes that surpass all understanding.

Growth is the key to find spiritual maturity with God. In your quiet moments begin to reflect on how you can start to rebirth yourself. Ask God who have He created you to be.

REFLECT

_____

_____

_____

_____

_____

YOUR PERSONAL PRAYER

_____

_____

_____

_____

_____

_____

_____

_____

_____

Psalm 138:8 ESV "The LORD will fulfill his purpose for me; your steadfast love, O LORD, endures forever. Do not forsake the work of your hands."

Fulfillment has not come

I must keep going even though my vision has not come yet.
I must remember it takes time.
God is in control.
Vision needs to rise, the crushing needs to be done.
My God is working something out for my good.
I must go to the crushing floor.
I must keep on waiting, waiting for my dreams to manifest.
I know my Lord will show up
My spirit cannot stay broken.
My fulfillment will be manifested on my knees.
Heavens are roaring to hear my testimony.
A testimony that bears witness, and pain.
Knowing that Jesus hears my prayer.
A prayer that is full of hope and promises.
Just waiting for his purpose to be fulfilled as He said.

When I immerse myself in the Word of God, I understand the importance of waiting. Trusting God fully and following His commandments ensures He is by my side in every aspect of my life. If God plants a desire or dream in my heart, I trust He will guide me to fulfill it, ensuring His glory shines through the process.

Open your heart, ask God to open the spirit of your mind to heard from him. His fulfillment is found in your waiting, in your surrender and in your obedience. Ask Him why your fulfillment has not come yet.

REFLECT

_____

_____

_____

_____

_____

YOUR PERSONAL PRAYER

_____

_____

_____

_____

_____

_____

_____

_____

_____

Romans 8:6-7 (NIV): "The mind governed by the flesh is death, but the mind governed by the Spirit is life and peace. The mind governed by the flesh is hostile to God; it does not submit to God's law, nor can it do so."

A carnal heart

Oh, Carnal mind where is your heart?
Is it of the flesh or is it of the spirit?
Oh, carnal mind how do you feel?
When I speak spiritual things of God.
Do you still do not understand?
Carnal mind do you have any revelation to give me?
Why are you fighting the spirit
Why are you not aligning up your thoughts and
actions with the principles of God?
Open up and see and believe.
Understanding what the heart is trying to express to you.
Understanding his ways, and believing what Jesus can do for you.
If you can believe spiritually.
Grow, read, and pray carnal mind.
The flesh has no power over you.
You are not alone, the battle will be won.
Stay strong and believe and you will see.

I personally recognize that the voice of the carnal mind comes from the flesh, constantly pulling me toward worldly desires. Yet, I know my mind is a precious gift from God and should not be wasted. I often feel a battle within me—one force guided by worldly desires and the other led by the Spirit of God. The question I ask myself is, which voice will I listen to? Will I align my thoughts with the principles of God, seeking His will and guidance, or will I be swayed by the principles of the world? As I go through my day, I reflect on where my thoughts are centered. Are they focused on God's truth, or are they consumed by worldly distractions?

This is a day-by-day struggle for everyone, but especially someone who is trying to walk with God. Our mind is so bombarded with the issues of life that we sometimes seek the things of the world instead of focusing on the truth of God. Ask God to help you to cultivate mindset that focus on eternal things rather than earthly concerns.

REFLECT

_____

_____

_____

_____

_____

_____

YOUR PERSONAL PRAYER

_____

_____

_____

_____

_____

_____

_____

_____

_____

_____

Psalm 139:1-4 (NIV): "You have searched me, Lord, and you know me. You know when I sit and when I rise; you perceive my thoughts from afar. You discern my going out and my lying down; you are familiar with all my ways. Before a word is on my tongue you, Lord, know it completely."

God never showed me

Imagine if God showed me my desire.
Imagine if God showed me my future.
Where would I be now?
My pride and my arrogance would make the best of me.
If God, never shows me my problems.
I would never know my hiccups.
He would never have showed me where I was going.
He knows where I start and where I am going to finish.
His protection is fierce over those he loves.
He will protects my destiny.
God knows why He shows me my hiccups and falls.
because he knows what will happen
He knows I will quit if I know and return to the familiar
My child he says, visions and dreams will come.
You are tested you will be refined until my will for you is fulfilled.
Nevertheless, my Lord, my time will come.
Knowing that God will show up in His time.

If God gave me everything I wanted exactly when I asked for it, I might not be where I am today. Sometimes, I feel the urge to take control, but I've realized that God desires me to do my part while trusting Him to shape me into someone who patiently waits for His perfect timing. I'm learning to take small, faithful steps and rely entirely on Jesus' sacrifice. God purposefully leaves some details of my life uncertain, and I believe this is for the best. It keeps me grounded in dependence on Him and reassures me of the greatness of His plan.

We repeatedly ask God why, especially when experiencing issues we cannot solve. Even in silence and delay, God still loves us. Sometimes, our answer does not come as we want, but waiting brings deeper understanding and transformation.

REFLECT

_____

_____

_____

_____

_____

YOUR PERSONAL PRAYER

_____

_____

_____

_____

_____

_____

_____

_____

_____

Psalm 56:8 NIV "You keep track of all my sorrows. You have collected all my tears in your bottle. You have recorded each one in your book."

Tears of mercy

The tears that I flow are for mercy.
mercy that my heart seeks.
The tears that I flow are for my peace.
A peace that brings life back to me.
The tears that I flow are for the wounds that I bear.
Wounds that I cannot heal.
The tears that I flow are for my service to serve.
A service that I cannot be a servant.
The tears that flow are in my hurt.
A hurt that can be removed.
The tears that I flow are for the pain.
A pain that only God can heal.
The tears that flow is from within.
A heart that is full of repentance.
The tears that flow is from regret.
A regret from what should have been.
The tears that I flow can teach me patience.
Patience to listen and wait on God.
The tears that I flow are to show God's love and mercy for me.
A bountiful of love that cannot be measured.

My trials and tribulations often bring me to tears. In these moments, I find strength, solace, and comfort by praying to God. I know He wants me to surrender everything to Him because He understands my pain completely. When I cry, it is a deeply personal declaration of my helplessness and a heartfelt plea for His mercy and grace.

God sees and values our tears especially when our heart is for Him. Reflect and journal down what you are feeling. Let your tears speak when you cannot utter the words.

REFLECT

_____

_____

_____

_____

_____

YOUR PERSONAL PRAYER

_____

_____

_____

_____

_____

_____

_____

_____

_____

1ST Corinthians 7:17 "Nevertheless, each person should live as a believer in whatever situation the Lord has assigned to them, just as God has called them. This is the rule I lay down in all the churches."

Jesus is calling us

Jesus is calling us to write.
He is calling us to rise.
Rise from the ashes.
To lose oppression and lack of hope.
He is calling you and me.
To open the doors and let him in.
Jesus say this is the way to go.
I know where I am taking you.
So, come and walk with me.
Shed off your fears and follow me.
The road is not easy, the climb can be rough.
The rocks and stones are there to stop you.
Do not be afraid.
I will catch you if you fall.
O come Jesus take my hand.
I will follow you.
I will fly with you wherever you go.

In 2004-2005, I felt God's call to change my life—a surreal and profoundly life-altering moment. That day became a significant turning point in my journey. The next day, I faced a test, but God showed up in my dream, reassuring me that He heard my prayers. The years followed were far from easy, filled with challenges, obstacles, and heartaches. Yet, through it all, something good always emerged, reminding me of His unwavering faithfulness and love.

> Does God have plans for each one of us? He is calling us to love others care for the poor and live our lives in such a way that we point to the power of his gospel.

REFLECT

_____

_____

_____

_____

_____

YOUR PERSONAL PRAYER

_____

_____

_____

_____

_____

_____

_____

_____

_____

_____

Isaiah 40:29 "He gives power to the faint, and to him who has no might he increases strength."

Emotional paralysis

When my past shows up.
Oh, how I wish I could pray.
To the one who can solve it all.
My emotions stand in limbo.
My mind is cluttered.
Fear of the past is arising again.
Doubt is not far behind.
My mind is frozen my decisions are in hostage.
Hold on tight, hold on tight look forward do not look back.
Fear and doubt cannot live here.
My limbs, my mind, my heart must be freed.
They must be set loose.
I will not be held hostage.
My future must come.
My excitement is in God.
My overflow I must follow.
God is in me I will not break I will not bend I will not fall.
Come arise oh, you of little faith.
Jesus is calling to set you free.

If you are someone paralyzed by fear, know that you are not alone. For me, the only way to overcome this is through prayer, faith, and asking God for the courage to break free from the fear that grips me. I thank God daily for His promises of redemption and healing, trusting that He will not only go before me but also guide each step I take on this journey. With Him, I know I am never walking alone.

Do you know that you can open your heart to God and share your feeling of emotional paralysis. It involves having faith, trust and patience and staying focus on God.

REFLECT

_____

_____

_____

_____

_____

YOUR PERSONAL PRAYER

_____

_____

_____

_____

_____

_____

_____

_____

Philippians 3:10 "That I may know Him and the power of His resurrection, and the fellowship of His sufferings, being conformed to His death,

He is Risen

Look at the sky and see the sun rising.
Saying a new day is coming.
The king is rising, rising for all to see.
A miracle is about to occur, the sun is rising quickly.
Come gather your things, the king is coming.
Your sins are forgiven, and the old laws that you obey are gone.
The king has risen to look into your heart.
He has fulfilled the law, change my people look at how you are suffering.
A new day is here, Jesus is risen.
Open your eyes my people announce to the crowd
and tell them that the king is risen.
Tell them that they are free.
A freedom that can never be brought.
Confidence to approach God boldly.
A direct access to God's throne.
O people come, receive what Jesus has brought for you.
Where you can receive mercy and find grace.
Come and see.

The overwhelming emotion I felt when I finally grasped the power of Christ's resurrection, and the magnitude of His sacrifice is beyond words. He became the ultimate offering for my salvation, and it is through His selfless act that I can stand here today. His promise of eternal life is the foundation of my Christian faith and continues to guide and shape my journey with Him.

How do you feel about the resurrected King Jesus and what He did for your life

REFLECT

_____

_____

_____

_____

_____

YOUR PERSONAL PRAYER

_____

_____

_____

_____

_____

_____

_____

_____

_____

_____

Jeremiah 29:12-13 "Then you will call upon Me and go and pray to and I will listen to you. And you will seek Me and find Me when you search for Me with all your heart.

A close Heart

God where did my heart go?
Why did my heart close?
Is it because of fear or is it because of anger?
I wonder my God why did my heart close?
I asked my God why I am not feeling his presence again.
Oh, God where did my heart go?
He said my daughter your heart is still there.
A heart that is filled with love to share.
A love that was born out of experience, for all to know.
Oh God listen to my close heart.
Open my heart I fear hope will go away please help my close heart.
Save me, save my heart, it needs to be opened.
My prayers shall only be for you Lord.
My life shall only be for you.
I bow only to you with a heart that is crying for you, my Lord.
Let my heart be acceptable to you.
A heart that is crying out for you, a heart that needs to be transformed.
A heart that can produce good fruits.
Bring joy out of my heart once again Lord.
My heart will not stay closed.
My heart will open again for your love to enter my Lord.

I went through a season in my faithful journey where I felt completely disconnected. It was as though my heart had shut down entirely. I experienced a deep emotional numbness, and even in church, hearing the word of God brought no response from me. This was profoundly stressful, and I came to realize that I needed to seek God more openly and intentionally, turning to Him spiritually to rekindle the connection I had lost.

Opening your heart and trying to connect to God is an ongoing process. Your feelings and perception sometimes get in the way and sometime the issues of life take over. How did you cope with this if it ever happens to you.

REFLECT

_____

_____

_____

_____

_____

_____

YOUR PERSONAL PRAYER

_____

_____

_____

_____

_____

_____

_____

_____

_____

Psalm 34:4-5 "I sought the Lord, and he answered me and delivered me from all my fears. Those who look to him are radiant, and their faces shall never be ashamed."

Lock up in silence

I remained broken, I could not hear my voice.
It was taken away by the trauma, the hurt, the pain,
the suffering and the sorrow. All was still there.
The challenges of my trauma I hid in the deepest part of my soul.
I could not bear to share it. I could not bear to announce it.
I knew I needed to wait in this time of distress.
I needed to hold on despite my pain.
I had to face my adversity, the brokenness I had to endure.
The burden I carry the dreams still I cherish in my heart
It was too much for me to bear.
Then suddenly my God heard my cry.
My praise broke through, and the padlock doors finally opened.
My pride changed to humility, and my hope rebuilt.
My God's made me stronger,
He breaks forth my voice for all to hear.
And birth a new me, for all to see.

This poem captures the deep trauma and hurt I endured during my early adult years. I was consumed by feelings of helplessness, failure, and rejection. The only glimmers of joy I could hold onto were thanking God for my children and the simple fact that I was still alive. During that time, I withdrew completely from the outside world, shutting myself off to cope. Yet, through it all, I never stopped praying. Even when I didn't understand why, prayer became my lifeline fragile yet unwavering thread of hope.

Have you ever felt a sense of hopelessness and thought that your life was a failure? How did you handle your feeling in your faith Journey

REFLECT

_____

_____

_____

_____

_____

YOUR PERSONAL PRAYER

_____

_____

_____

_____

_____

_____

_____

_____

_____

Psalm 71:20, "Though you have made me see troubles, many and bitter, you will restore my life again; from the depths of the earth, you will again bring me up".

It's ok to hold on while the tears still flow

I have I sat on my bed thinking why do I feel abundant?
My tears could not stop flowing.
Thinking that God abundant me.
Thinking Jesus does not need me anymore.
Thinking how can humanity be so evil.
As my tears kept flowing, hoping that the hands of
Jesus would stop my tears from flowing.
A feeling of despair gripped my mind, fear of the unknown
stood like a ring of darkness beyond my imagination.
Voices saying God is fed up with you.
He does not want you anymore.
Tears kept flowing like a river going downstream.
Amid the tears, hope was still there.
A small voice kept telling me to hold on.
My tears welled up in my eyes, my throat felt like it was closing.
My heart hurts, weighing like a burden of rocks piling up.
A burden that only Jesus can take away and bring back a life full of joy.
Knowing that there is a wealth of hope waiting for me.
His peace and love come to wipe away my tears forever.

Over the years, I've shed countless tears, yet I've learned to channel them into prayers for hope and comfort. Through this process, I've discovered healing and restoration in ways I never imagined possible.

How does crying out to God help you heal. Journal your experience.

REFLECT

_____

_____

_____

_____

_____

_____

YOUR PERSONAL PRAYER

_____

_____

_____

_____

_____

_____

_____

_____

_____

_____

_____

Isaiah 55:11: "So is my word that goes out from my mouth: It will not return to me empty but will accomplish what I desire and achieve the purpose for which I sent it."

Life Giving Words

Do you know God's words is life giving?
O people of little faith, wake up, look up.
God's word brings life, life that cannot be destroyed.
Learning his words and speaking it, will change your life.
Oh, people of God, people who are unsure, people who are undecided.
Listen up God's words is what we need.
If we believe in his words, light will enter.
A light that we have never seen,
Darkness will go as light enters in.
His words are life giving and can bring you back from death.
So, people of God be zealous for his word.
Constantly seeking him, so that your story can change.
Open invite him in, not be ashamed, He does not lie.
If you love his word, He will always be your God.
Rejection is not part of his instruction.
Open the door and enter, for he is waiting.
His words are alive, all he asked is to accept
him and obey his commandments.
Remembering his word can bring life back that was lost.

God's Word is alive and accessible to me whenever I read it. Opening my heart to its teachings gives me the guidance and wisdom I need to follow His plans and purposes for my life.

God's living word is alive and available for all to read. Does God's word speak to your heart? Explain in your journal how you felt when read or hear the word of God.

REFLECT

_____

_____

_____

_____

_____

_____

YOUR PERSONAL PRAYER

_____

_____

_____

_____

_____

_____

_____

_____

_____

_____

Psalm 42:1 says, "As the deer pants for streams of water, so my soul pants for you, O God".

Longing for intimacy with God

O lord where did my thirst go for you my first love.
I long for the intimacy that I had as a child,
I long for the God I spoke to with my grand aunt.
In my silence I struggle for a personal unique connection with you.
Desiring to experience your presence in a tangible way
Is in these times that my heart yearns for you, my Lord.
It is in these times that my hope leaps out for joy.
A joy that only you can fill.
Times have past, for me but not for you God.
I know my journey with you will never end.
Because I know that you will never stop loving me.
A submission that only you can understand.
A life that begins with love, a love that I cannot fathom.
But only you know what total intimacy with you really means.
Father God, I yearn for that intimacy and
that will bring spiritual maturity.
I do not want to be a stranger in my own thoughts.
I want you to dwell within me, bringing a deep and lasting intimacy.

I composed this poem during a fast devoted to the theme "Thirsting for God." The deep longing and confusion I experienced led me to fully surrender, seeking a more personal and spiritual connection with Him. I yearn for the closeness He so desires to share with me.

Requesting a greater intimacy with God should be heartfelt and encouraging. Have you ever felt you needed more intimacy with God, a closer relationship with him. Journal your thoughts.

REFLECT

_____

_____

_____

_____

_____

_____

YOUR PERSONAL PRAYER

_____

_____

_____

_____

_____

_____

_____

_____

_____

_____

Isaiah 40:31 says, "But they that wait upon the Lord shall renew their strength; they shall mount up with wings like eagles; they shall run, and not be weary; and they shall walk, and not faint"

Soaring Upward

Where are my wings for me to fly.
I need to soar higher than ever before.
I need the wind to blow and guide me to my upward calling.
My wings are waiting for your direction, when to flap them.
Waiting for the wind to become stronger so that I can glide upward.
Oh, do I wait for the helper so that He can guide and direct me.
I know He can raise me up, to soar in His presence.
As high as I can go.
Soaring for something better by fixing my
eyes and thoughts upon my Lord.
Rising above life's challenges, limitations and struggles.
Rising with your divine strength for my perspective and purpose.
Always relying on your strength which is limitless
so that I can soar like an eagle.
To higher heights and endless possibilities.

Trusting God's power to carry me beyond disappointments and challenges is a genuinely uplifting thought. When I fly, I sometimes imagine angels' wings supporting the plane as it soars through the sky. This visualization reassures me that God, my Creator, is in control—not the pilot, the air, or the wind. The act of soaring symbolizes that as I cultivate a deeper relationship with Him, I can experience favor and blessings beyond what I ever thought possible.

How can soaring high brings favor and prosperity from God. Journal your thoughts.

REFLECT

_____

_____

_____

_____

_____

YOUR PERSONAL PRAYER

_____

_____

_____

_____

_____

_____

_____

_____

_____

_____

1st Kings 8:61: Let your heart therefore be loyal to the LORD our God, to walk in His statutes and keep His commandments, as at this day."

Where is your Allegiance

Saints of God, who do you pledge your allegiance to.
Is it your children or your Home
Is it your Job or your finance.
Is it your food or you're craving for junk.
Is it in social media or others.
Oh, saints of God, remember the one who gave your life.
The one who gave you his commandments and his statues.
So that it can guide you along the right part.
Where is your loyalty saints of God.
Don't you remember the scriptures that He freely gave you.
Don't you remember you can go to him without fear.
When is the last time you have fellowship with Him.
When is the last time you listen to his voice.
Oh, saints of God, stay align with Him.
Stay in a relationship with Him.
His covenant is forever, and His love is unconditional.
So, keep your heart aligned with Him.
So that you can stay allegiance to his calling.

As I listened to my pastor ask, "Is my allegiance truly to God?" I began to ponder the depth of my commitment. Am I genuinely loyal to Him, even when life becomes difficult? Am I faithful to the Cross of Jesus in the face of challenges? I realized that to truly honor my allegiance, I must prioritize my relationship with God above everything else. This means living a life aligned with His values, no matter what obstacles I encounter.

Pray and ask God for you to stay vigilant against distraction, temptations and influences. Reflect on how you can stay focused.

REFLECT

_____

_____

_____

_____

_____

YOUR PERSONAL PRAYER

_____

_____

_____

_____

_____

_____

_____

_____

_____

Printed in the United States
by Baker & Taylor Publisher Services